Identity vs Reality

Overcoming Rejection and Reclaiming Your Crown

GLACIA K. SIMPSON

DAYELight

PUBLISHERS

ISBN: 978-1-966723-42-4 (paperback)

Table of Contents

Official Introduction

*I*dentity vs. Reality: Overcoming Rejection and Reclaiming Your Crown delves into the complexities of self-worth, identity, and spiritual healing. Authored with a deep understanding of the struggles faced by individuals dealing with rejection, the book invites readers to explore the transformative power of Christ's love in reclaiming their identity.

The book highlights the contrast between the false identity shaped by external circumstances such as rejection, abandonment, or societal expectations and the identity found in God's perspective. It challenges readers to look beyond worldly labels and to root their sense of worth and value in God's truth. The title itself "Identity vs. Reality" calls attention to the internal battle many face, where feelings of inadequacy and rejection clash with the reality of God's promises and unconditional love.

Throughout the book, readers are encouraged to confront past wounds, let go of negative self-perceptions, and embrace the truth of who they are in Christ.

Ultimately, **Identity vs. Reality** seeks to help individuals overcome the lies that hinder their spiritual growth and prevent them from stepping into the fullness of their God-given potential. The message is one of hope and empowerment, reminding believers that they are crowned with glory and honour in Christ, and no amount of rejection can diminish the love and purpose that God has for them.

IVR Playlist

These are songs that helped me get through the writing process. I hope they bless you as they've blessed me. Enjoy!

He Understands, What I Needed, Most Beautiful, On Time God - ***Chandler Moore***

Only You Can Satisfy - ***William McDonald***

Drink Offering, Another Surrender, The Story I'll Tell, Evidence - ***Naomi Raine***

Validation Album - ***JohnMark Wiggan***

Nothing But Goodness, The Good Shepherd - ***Joe L. Barnes***

Abba, Take Me Back, Real Thing - ***Dante Bowe***

Make Room, Cycles, Detail, Grace - ***Jonathan McReynolds***

Reckless Love - ***Cory Asbury***

*The Kingdom Is Yours, He Has Time - **Common Hymnal***

*Lord, You Are Good, He Won't Fail, You Remain, Fear is Not My Future - **Todd Galberth***

*House Of God - **Mercy Culture Worship***

*Sing Over Me - **Dunsin Oyekan***

*Show Me Your Face, Let the Alabaster Break - **Red Worship, Lizzie Morgan***

*Constant, Stand Still, New Wine - **Maverick City***

*Sold Out, Song of Obedience - **Junior Tucker***

*Again - **Kirk Franklin***

*Tethered - **Sinmidele***

*No Bondage - **Jubilee Worship***

*Yahweh - Live - **Transformation Worship***

*You Waited, Be Still, Intentional, Easter - **Travis Greene***

Chapter 1

The Struggle Between Identity and Reality

From the moment we take our first breath, our sense of self is subjected to the mood and trends of the world, shaping our perception of who we are. Family, culture, experiences, and even our failures whisper definitions of our worth and purpose. Get a career, marry, have kids in a house with a white picket fence.

However, what the world says about us often conflicts with the truth of who God says we are. This battle between identity and reality is one of the greatest struggles we face.

THE TRAP OF REJECTION

Rejection is one of the most painful experiences we can encounter. No matter the source, it can leave wounds that can taint and alter our very being. It convinces us that our worth can be manipulated.

It tells us, we don't deserve the gifts, opportunities or even the peace that we receive. We are deemed unworthy of love and all the beauties this life has to offer.

Let me encourage you, even Jesus faced rejection. He was despised and rejected by the very people he came to die for. Yet, He never allowed the opinions of those around Him to define who He was and is—the Son of God, Savior, Redeemer, Lord and the list goes on.

In a world where many have no sense of self and search for themselves in whatever seems the most appetizing, it is my hope that this book will be a tool in assisting persons to find their identity in God.

THE POWER OF PERCEPTION

Many of us have been conditioned to see ourselves through the lens of rejection, past wounds, and societal expectations. We wear labels imposed upon us—labels of failure, insignificance, or inadequacy—especially when life repeatedly reinforces these negative perceptions, they become our reality. However, reality, as we perceive it, is not always true.

The enemy works tirelessly to distort our view of ourselves, making us believe that we are unworthy, unloved, or incapable. But God's Word tells a different story. He calls us chosen, beloved, and victorious. The question we must ask ourselves is: Which voice will we believe?

And do not be conformed to this world [any longer with its superficial values and customs], but be transformed and progressively changed [as you mature spiritually] by the renewing of your mind [focusing on godly values and ethical attitudes], so that you may prove [for yourselves] what the will of God is, that which is good and acceptable and perfect [in His plan and purpose for you].
Romans 12:2 AMP

The journey of overcoming rejection begins with a shift in perspective. We must choose to see ourselves as God sees us, not as the world has labelled us or how we have labelled ourselves.

For most of my life, I operated as whatever and whoever others needed me to be. My favourite colour was whatever that of the person I liked had as their own. My emotions were regulated by those around me. I made up people in my mind and called them my different personalities just to make me not feel alone.

Ask me what my aspirations were, and I'd tell you what I thought would garner me the most impressive looks and nods of approval. Glacia was a construct, not a person.

It took years of the Holy Spirit—often dragging me, kicking and screaming, fighting self-hatred—to learn to allow myself to be loved correctly and intentionally. This was because healing can be such a pain in the butt, especially, when you have no idea what the end will look like.

Our reality, experiences, culture, struggles, and environment often influence how we regard our identity in Christ. The Bible teaches that our identity in Christ is rooted in His finished work, not in our circumstances.

WAYS REALITY AFFECTS OUR IDENTITY IN CHRIST

1. *Circumstances and Struggles* – Hardships, disappointments, and even successes can cause us to question or lose sight of our actual identity in Christ. However, Scripture reminds us that we are "more than conquerors" (Romans 8:37) and that nothing can separate us from God's love (Romans 8:38–39).

2. *Past Experiences and Wounds* – Trauma, rejection, or sin remain the highest contributing factors to us creating false identities, but in Christ, we are made new (2 Corinthians 5:17), forgiven (Ephesians 1:7), and healed (Isaiah 53:5).

3. *Culture and Society* – The world's values and God's truths are always at odds. This often poses a challenge for us to live out our faith. Society may define worth by achievements or appearance, but God defines us as loved and chosen (Ephesians 1:4-5).

I have told you these things, so that in Me you may have [perfect] peace. In the world you have

*tribulation and distress and suffering, but be
courageous [be confident, be undaunted, be filled
with joy]; I have overcome the world." [My
conquest is accomplished, My victory abiding.]*
John 16:33 AMP

While our reality can challenge our identity in Christ, it does not define it. Our identity is anchored in God's unchanging love and truth. Identity is crucial in the Kingdom of God because it determines how we see ourselves, how we relate to each other, our response or obedience to God, and how we fulfil our purpose.

If we don't know who we are in Christ, we struggle to approach the throne of grace boldly. Our internal battles cause us to miss the mark, but, when we embrace our identity as His children, we grow in intimacy with Him, knowing we are fully accepted and loved. (Ephesians 1:5).

It is my earnest desire that at the end of this read, you will understand and accept the victory you have in Jesus—that greater is He who is in you, who emboldens you to overcome rejection and reclaim your crown.

Journal Prompts

1. Where have you let your reality (circumstances, upbringing, or trauma) define your identity more than the Word of God?

2. What moments in your life caused you to question who you really are?

3. Ask God to reveal: *"What lies about myself have I believed that You had never spoken?"*

Reflection

_____

_____

_____

_____

_____

_____

_____

_____

_____

Identity vs Reality

Chapter 2

Man in the Mirror

Do you recall the famous Michael Jackson song: 'Man in the Mirror'? Who do you see when you look in the mirror? Do you see a child of God: fearfully and wonderfully made or do you see someone defined by past mistakes, rejection, and self-doubt? Too often, the reflection we perceive is distorted by the wounds of our past and the lies of the enemy.

One of the biggest hurdles I had to conquer in this journey with Christ was my never ending imposter syndrome and self-loathing. Those who know me will tell you one of two things: I am either the most outgoing and charming person they know or horrifically hard on myself. Both things could be true at any time of the day.

I was a professional social chameleon. If someone, whether relational or otherwise showed any form of interest in me then I'd become exactly who they wanted. It didn't matter if it went against my beliefs or feelings. Someone else's approval always outweighed my inner turmoil. I had no clear view of who I was, much less whose I was.

For as long as I could remember I rooted my identity in the expectations others had of me. If I laughed too loud for you, I'd be as quiet as a mouse. My thoughts were too out of the box? Who needs personal opinions anyway?

I was the child my family didn't have to worry about because 'I had my head on my body' or 'the younger ones just needed more attention' and 'I should understand'. Somewhere along those lines what seemed like trust, turned into emotional and mental neglect. What was I to do, though? I was expected to take care of myself, and that's what I did. Without noticing that neglect as a young child allowed me to seek attention elsewhere. I fell right into the arms of two child predators between the ages of 4 and 11 years.

That experience would later shape my mind for the rest of my adolescent life. I wanted to be loved, and to be loved I needed to be desirable in whatever form it took. So, I presented myself as such. If I could gain their attention, maybe they'd deem me worthy of the love and affection I so deeply longed for.

For if anyone only listens to the word without obeying it, he is like a man who looks very carefully at his natural face in a mirror; for once he has looked at himself and gone away, he immediately forgets what he looked like.
James 1:23-24 AMP

The world teaches us to judge ourselves by our accomplishments, outward appearances, and other people's opinions. We start to internalise a false identity that is based on fear and insecurity. This cycle that James 1:23-24 speaks of is one that many of us live in—looking at our God-given identities but then reverting to the distorted perceptions imposed by our experiences.

As I grew, so did my insecurities and the need for validation. This resulted in me no longer finding myself worthy of anything 'good' because if I wasn't affirmed by someone else then I was obviously failing and doing a horrible job. Right?

Looking back, I imagined how much it must have broken God's heart to see me reduce myself to nothing more than eye candy or a puppet for any willing bystander. However, that was the perception I had of myself.

So, God created man in His own image, in the image and likeness of God He created him; male and female He created them.
Genesis 1:27 AMP

See yourself as God sees you—created in His image, after His likeness.

Everything changes when you start to view yourself as God does. You are no longer bound by other people's views. Your past mistakes no longer determine who you are. Rather, you move with the assurance that you are a child of the one true King.

Allow the word of God to be your mirror. Allow the One who knows you, formed you, to be the only reflection of your worth. You will see yourself as He sees you; redeemed, loved, and as royalty—when He is your mirror.

BREAKING FREE FROM A DISTORTED REFLECTION

As we seek freedom from a twisted reflection, it is a necessity that we have the right framework in place to allow us to see the true picture. We must challenge and replace the false perceptions we have allowed ourselves to accept.

If you are seeking their approval your identity becomes rooted in their validation and applause. When there is no standing ovation, then what?

1. *Recognize the Lies:* The enemy seeks to distort your identity with deception. What voices have you been listening to? Do they align with God's truth?

_____

_____

_____

_____

_____

_____

_____

2. *Replace with Truth:* God's Word is the only mirror that reflects your true self. Meditate on scriptures that declare your worth. Here are a few scriptures you can use to affirm yourself.

- *"For we are His workmanship [His own master work, a work of art], created in Christ Jesus [reborn from above spiritually transformed, renewed, ready to be used] for good works, which God prepared [for us] beforehand [taking paths which He set], so that we would walk in them [living the good life which He prearranged and made ready for us]." **Eph. 2:10***

- *Therefore if anyone is in Christ [that is, grafted in, joined to Him by faith in Him as Saviour], he is a new creature [reborn and renewed by the Holy Spirit]; the old things [the previous moral and spiritual condition] have passed away. Behold, new things have come [because spiritual awakening brings a new life]. **2 Cor. 5:17***

- *But you are a chosen race, a royal priesthood, a consecrated nation, a [special] people for God's own possession, so that you may proclaim the excellences [the wonderful deeds and virtues and perfections] of Him who called you out of darkness into His marvellous light. 1 Peter 2:9*

3. *Walk in Confidence:* Transformation comes when we not only believe but also act according to our God-given identity. Reject the shame of the past and embrace the calling God has placed on your life. What has He called you to do that rejection has caused you to cast aside? Write them here.

_____

_____

_____

_____

_____

_____

_____

_____

_____

_____

_____

Journal Prompts

1. What do you see when you look in the mirror and how do you feel?

2. Whose voice has shaped your self-perception the most: God's, your own, or others'?

3. Invite God into this reflection: *"Show me who I truly am in You. Not who I pretend to be, or who I've been told I am."*

Reflection

_____

_____

_____

_____

_____

_____

_____

_____

Chapter 3

Good Grief: The Thorns and Thistles of Life

One day I was in a counseling session with my pastor, and he said these words to me. *"Your Identity isn't rooted in your ability to endure suffering".* At some point in life, we've all experienced some level of grief, whether it was the loss of a friendship, parent or a significant other.

In Genesis 3, God tells Adam that the ground will be cursed because of his sin, and that it will produce "thorns and thistles." This is a representation of the struggles that all of us would face with sin, suffering, and a broken world.

Grief immobilized me for years. It felt like I was stuck in a cycle of loss—romantic relationships, family, friendships etc. There was a new level of grief associated with every lesson that I needed to learn. Regrettably, time waits on no man and it seemed as if I didn't have an option to slow down and deal with it.

Vulnerability wasn't my strongest suit, and grief was forcing me to be exactly that. I hated tears. I believed they were the biggest sign of weakness, and I couldn't afford to be weak. As the eldest daughter in my family, a lot was required of me whether I had it in me to be strong or not, especially during the time of my mother's passing in 2021.

My mom had fallen ill over the period of two weeks. It wasn't as if she hadn't been ill before, so like always, I expected her to pull through. I recall that Saturday night like my own name. My entire family was cooped up in my grandmother's room laughing while my aunt, uncle and I were cleaning my mom. She placed a small kiss on my aunt's neck which made her chuckle. Then without warning she collapsed and she and I were on the floor with her head in my lap.

Everyone was scrambling, unsure of what to do. As I held her on my lap and did my best to talk to her, it was as if we had traded roles. I was the mother praying for my child to be ok. Nothing felt real to me. I remember praying and begging God to sustain her, keep her going. I told Him that it wasn't her time because our relationship was finally beginning to grow. It was not His will. I felt abandoned. Abandoned by my mother and rejected by God.

I prayed to the Lord, asking Him to save her. I asked Him to release her from her pain. Why? Would He take her from me? These were the thoughts that flooded my mind amidst me feigning strength during her burial process.

"Jesus Wept."
John 11:35 AMP

The shortest verse in the Bible, yet one of the most powerful if you ask me. Jesus—God in the flesh; Creator, Deliverer, the Redeemer—wept. For context, this is after Jesus found out that a beloved friend of his, Lazarus, had passed. The same Jesus that knew He was going to resurrect Lazarus, wept.

I wonder if when Joseph, Jesus' earthly father, was dying, Jesus asked God for permission to save him? Did God deny Him of that request?

I wonder if Jesus bargained, interceded, lamented, but eventually came to terms with the Lord's decision like David did concerning his child with

Bathsheba. I consider this because we often blame God when things don't go our way and say He's this and that, and He doesn't understand how we feel. But Jesus is His son. Jesus, though He understood the assignment, endured the same if not more heartbreaks, just like we do.

He could raise Lazarus but not 'save' John (his cousin) or Joseph. It is in these times of uncertainty when we must be anchored in our identity, to remind ourselves that our purpose is not ours to always comprehend, but to submit to God's will.

It is ok for us to have certain feelings, but not to be consumed and blinded by them.

We are mere flesh. There will be death and life. Seasons change. Trees will bear beautifully in spring and look like a hollow version of themselves in autumn. Does it hurt any less? Of course not. Did it make me miraculously stop missing my mom? Not. One. Bit! It did, however, give me a better understanding of His love and sovereignty.

This is in no way diminishing the earth-shattering effects grief can have. We all process emotions and experiences differently. I advocate for therapy and counselling because it's hard to be effective when your heart and soul are in shambles. Seek wise counsel.

The God who gives also takes but He will hold us through every life altering moment as long as we allow Him.

"Blessed [forgiven, refreshed by God's grace] are those who mourn [over their sins and repent], for they will be comforted [when the burden of sin is lifted]."
Matthew 5:4 AMP

Grief looks different to everyone. Some have lost loved ones to death. For others, it was relationships they never thought would end, dreams that were never accomplished, broken friendships, parents that chose not to be parents, and the most hidden version—that broken child you've been harbouring inside that has been searching for love and release.

Give yourself the grace to grieve; the space to exist in between hurting and healing. It's all a part of the ebb and flow of life. It's okay to step out of the performance and unravel. If you don't allow yourself that time to mourn whatever has been weighing on your heart, it will come back with an even greater force and can damage you.

29

There is goodness in your grieving process. Do not hide from it. He hasn't called you to isolate you in shame and hurt, but to insulate you with his joy and peace. If He brought you to it, He shall bring you through it, but only if you let Him. It's hard to trust and hope when you've been disappointed, especially when that disappointment is directed to God.

Emotions are vying for the God spot in your hearts. They fight to become the truth that you live by. They are not. In the moment, they creep into your bones and cripple you. They paint the narrative of truth when that's not the case. Emotions are good but they must be governed by the word of God.

"He was despised and rejected by men, A Man of sorrows and pain and acquainted with grief; And like One from whom men hide their faces He was despised, and we did not appreciate His worth or esteem Him."
Isaiah 53:3 AMP

A man of sorrows and pain, well acquainted with grief. Imagine, The King of the Universe, The Lord of Lords who wants for nothing because all things come from Him, is acquainted with grief; my grief, your grief. His beloved cousin was beheaded because of Him. His earthly father died. His friend passed away, and He had to wait until an appointed time just to bring about His father's glory, so that those around Him would believe.

Though many people view grieving as something to avoid or something that simply causes sorrow, when seen through the lens of our identity in Christ, grief can become an insightful experience. It is a journey of recovery and transformation that provides a greater understanding of God's consolation, love, and the hope we have in Him. Grieving may be a key part of discovering who we really are in Christ, resulting in recovery, development, and a closer relationship with Him.

Now we do not want you to be uninformed, believers, about those who are asleep [in death], so that you will not grieve [for them] as the others do who have no hope [beyond this present life].
1 Thessalonians 4:13 AMP

For the Christian, grief does not have the final word. While it is overwhelming in the moment, we are not without hope. Paul reminds us of this in 1 Thessalonians 4:13. As believers, we grieve with hope, knowing that our sorrow will one day be turned to joy. This hope is found in the resurrection of Jesus

Christ, who conquered death and promises eternal life for those who believe in Him.

Our grief is temporary, but the joy that comes with eternal life in Christ is forever. As we grieve, we do so with the assurance that one day all things will be made new. In the meantime, we hold on to the hope that God is with us in our sorrow, and He will bring comfort and healing in His perfect time.

Revelation 21:4 gives us a beautiful picture of the hope we have in Christ: "*and He will wipe away every tear from their eyes; and there will no longer be death; there will no longer be sorrow and anguish, or crying, or pain; for the former order of things has passed away.*" This is the ultimate comfort in our grief—the promise of eternal restoration, where all the pain, sorrow, and loss we experience in this life will be completely wiped away.

Here are a few pertinent questions: "Where does our identity lie? Is it in our emotions that change like the weather or our High Priest who is familiar with our grief?

Ultimately, good grief is not about avoiding pain but about embracing the process of healing that leads to a greater understanding of who we are in Christ and the hope that we have in Him. As we navigate grief, we do so with the knowledge that God is with us, working all things together for our good and His glory (Romans 8:28).

Take a moment and place these concerns/feelings at his feet.

- *For to me, to live is Christ [He is my source of joy, my reason to live] and to die is gain [for I will be with Him in eternity].* **Psalm 73:26**

- *So, for now you are in grief; but I will see you again, and [then] your hearts will rejoice, and no one will take away from you your [great] joy.* **John 16:22**

- *I can do all things [which He has called me to do] through Him who strengthens and empowers me [to fulfil His purpose I am self-sufficient in Christ's sufficiency; I am ready for anything and equal to anything through Him who infuses me with inner strength and confident peace.]* **Philippians 4:13**

- *and He will wipe away every tear from their eyes; and there will no longer be death; there will no longer be sorrow and anguish, or crying, or pain; for the [a]former order of things has passed away." **Revelation 21:4***

- *For I consider [from the standpoint of faith] that the sufferings of the present life are not worthy to be compared with the glory that is about to be revealed to us and in us! **Romans 8:18***

- *The Lord is near to the heartbroken and He saves those who are crushed in spirit (contrite in heart, truly sorry for their sin) **Psalm 34:18***

- *My flesh and my heart may fail, but God is the rock and strength of my heart and my portion forever. **Psalm 73:26***

Journal Prompts

1. What grief or loss have you suffered and not fully processed?

2. How have thorns from your past hardened your heart or distorted your identity?

3. What would it look like to surrender that grief to God and allow Him to grow something beautiful from it?

Reflection

_____

_____

_____

_____

_____

_____

_____

_____

_____

_____

Identity vs Reality

Chapter 4

Gracefully Broken

To be "gracefully broken" may seem self-contradictory at first. How can something broken also be graceful? Yet, this is the beauty of our faith, the concept that through our brokenness, God's grace is most evident, and it is in our weakness that His strength is made perfect.

When I was 17, I co-wrote my first book called 'Living A Royal Reality: Teen Edition Vol 1', along with 10 other amazing girls.

Yes, this is a shameless plug. Yes, I recommend you read it.

At the time, I thought that was the most vulnerable I would ever be and that my past was the epitome of my suffering and confusion. Lord knows, I could have not been more wrong! The past seven years utterly exhausted any and everything I had in me. They were, single-handedly, my most transitional years. Good, bad and in-between. These years have demanded so much of me. I can't tell you how many times I have thrown in the towel and had it thrown back in my face and told "drink some tea, a gas" and had to keep the ball rolling.

I somehow battled with my faith more than I had while living in the world. It felt like I was stuck in a constant cycle of "Yes, I'm finally over this" and crying my heart out because "God, I thought we were over this".

I grew tired of sounding like a broken record. It was as if no matter how much I thought I had grown and how much I had overcome, there was still so much left to deal with. It was exhausting. I was tired of the cycles, tired of shame and guilt. I was tired of my brokenness.

Through all this inner turmoil I learnt 2 things:

1. Being 'Gracefully Broken' means allowing God to work through our pains, failures, and imperfections, using them as instruments of transformation and healing. It's about surrendering our brokenness to God and trusting that He can bring beauty from the shattered pieces of our lives.

2. God uses 'broken' people.

*My [only] sacrifice [acceptable] to God is a broken
spirit; A broken and contrite heart [broken with
sorrow for sin, thoroughly penitent], such, O God,
you will not despise.*
Psalm 51:17 AMP

We live in a broken world, one marked by pain, loss,
and suffering. From the moment Adam and Eve
sinned, brokenness entered the world, affecting every
aspect of our lives. Relationships are fractured,
bodies grow ill, hearts are wounded, and dreams are
shattered.

But brokenness isn't just a result of their decision;
it's also an essential part of the believer's journey.
Jesus Himself was "broken" for us. On the cross, He
endured unimaginable pain and suffering to redeem
us from the consequences of sin. His body was
broken, His blood was shed, and through His
sacrifice, our brokenness is made whole.

How many times have we tried to carry the weight of
the world on our shoulders but all it did was burden
and break our hearts, minds and spirit?

I'll let you in on a little secret.

You are not bionic. You don't run on oil and batteries. You're actually human, with real struggles, problems and pain. Blood flows through your veins and a heart beats in your chest. The Word tells us that *"in this world we will have many trials but take heart; for Jesus has overcome the world"* (John 16v33). The same Jesus who said those words, His spirit lives in you. He wants to dwell in and with you if you'd allow Him.

Brokenness is not something we can avoid; it is a part of the human experience. But we are invited to bring our brokenness to God and allow Him to work through it, making us whole in ways we never thought possible.

In the world's eyes, brokenness is something to be feared or hidden, a weakness to be ashamed of. Yet, in God's Kingdom, brokenness is a place of beauty. Just as a potter takes clay and molds it into something beautiful after breaking it down, God takes the shattered pieces of our lives and shapes them into something far more glorious than we could ever imagine.

Jesus is the only reason I'm alive. Some days are a fight between where He's leading me and the suffocation of phantom's past. There were nights when I silently screamed into my pillow wondering why I was only a free test trial and never a full-time commitment. There were days when I was laughing and talking with people, yet I was choking back tears because I didn't want anyone to know how broken and violated I felt inside.

I didn't know I needed saving until I came face to face with my brokenness.

What you feel pales in comparison to who God is calling you to be—who he knitted in your mother's womb. It will take some breaking and bending. It will hurt and have you question if following Jesus was the right decision. From one trying soul to the next, I can tell you that though the road is rocky and the eyes are droopy, the Lord sustains.

saying, "Father, if You are willing, remove this cup [of divine wrath] from Me; yet not My will, but [always] Yours be done."
Luke 22:42 AMP
The first step in becoming gracefully broken is to surrender. To surrender means acknowledging our brokenness and allowing God to work in us. It means

releasing control, admitting that we cannot fix ourselves, and trusting that God can heal, restore, and use our pain for His glory.

The story of Jesus in the Garden of Gethsemane shows us the ultimate act of surrender. In His most vulnerable moment, Jesus prayed. This prayer of surrender was not just a moment of obedience; it was the key to His mission of redemption. Similarly, our brokenness is an opportunity to surrender our will to God's and trust that He will use our pain for a greater purpose.

Our brokenness does not define us, but it is part of our story. We are not perfect and we don't need to pretend to be. When we accept that we are gracefully broken, we live with humility, compassion, and grace toward others. We recognize that everyone is walking through a journey of brokenness and healing.

The process of healing often begins with brokenness. We cannot experience true restoration without first acknowledging the areas where we are broken. There is no 'final level' to growth and healing. There will always be something new to uncover and learn.

Acknowledge the fact that it hurts. Acknowledge the fact that it broke you. Cry. Mourn. Grieve. Kick and scream but present all these emotions to Jesus.

We often recite the scripture "Forgive 70 times 7", but in that same Bible it says love God and love thy neighbour as thyself. If we are to love and forgive that same neighbour who has hurt, offended, rejected and scorned us; then doesn't it also mean that to forgive them, we must first forgive ourselves?

I don't know about you but that was always where I faltered because it just seemed too heavy. Listen, no part of you is innately bad. Every ounce of your being attempts to protect you, though the methods may remain quite questionable.

As we walk through our own experiences of brokenness, we can find comfort and hope in knowing that Jesus understands. His grace is sufficient, and His love is unwavering. Our brokenness is not the end of the story—it is the beginning of a beautiful transformation as we allow God to work through it.

Gracefully broken, we are made whole, not by our own strength, but by the grace and power of God working in and through our weaknesses.

It is my prayer that you learn how to master your emotions. They are not the god of your life. Your Creator, Savior and King expects you to do nothing but be who you are in this moment, because who you are now doesn't have to be who you are later.

Journal Prompts

1. When was the last time you experienced a breaking that felt unbearable, but now you are able to see God's grace in it?

2. How is God using your brokenness to make room for your true identity?

3. Ask the Lord: *"What is being restored in me through the breaking?"*

Reflection

_____

_____

_____

_____

_____

_____

_____

_____

_____

_____

Identity vs Reality

Chapter 5

Beauty in Vulnerability

"Vulnerability is often most difficult for the strong. Your identity isn't based on how strong you pretend to be."

This book almost didn't happen. When God told me what it truly was about, I wondered if I was going crazy and hearing voices. How could He expect me to bare my heart and soul to a bunch of random people? What will my family think when they've heard of all the mess I've been through? Will my church family look at me differently? Would my friends feel betrayed?

All these thoughts ran through my mind because I was scared. Though the sight of a lizard or flying cockroach does strike the fear of God into me, my biggest fear in life has always been to allow someone to see me—the real me—without walls, without defence.

I was always the girl behind the camera or hidden in the background for choir. Any attempt I made at trying to be front and centre was either because I wanted the wrong kind of attention or to feel worthy of what I thought love was. This, however, is a completely different ball game. We often dilute our identity with circumstances we've been through, people we've met, or words we've said. These are indications of who we are at our core.

Vulnerability is often seen as a weakness in today's world. A place where we open ourselves to hurt, disappointment, and rejection. But when it comes to our identity in Christ, vulnerability is not only a strength, it is the place where God's grace and beauty shine most brightly. It is in our weakness and openness that we truly experience God's love, healing, and transformation.

As the first daughter, granddaughter, niece etc. in my family, a lot of responsibility was placed on me at a young age. I didn't have time to cry about it. I didn't have time to say "Hi, I'm in pain, do you see me?" I couldn't falter. It wasn't a part of the job description.

"but He has said to me, "My grace is sufficient for you [My lovingkindness and My mercy are more than enough always available regardless of the

situation]; for [My] power is being perfected [and is completed and shows itself most effectively] in [your] weakness." Therefore, I will all the more gladly boast in my weaknesses, so that the power of Christ [may completely enfold me and] may dwell in me."

2 Corinthians 12:9 AMP

Paul reveals the truth that vulnerability is not a liability but a gateway to divine strength. It is in our vulnerabilities that we invite God's power to work in our lives, refining us and revealing His glory through our brokenness.

In a world that values strength, success, and self-sufficiency, vulnerability can feel like a threat. We often associate it with exposure to rejection, judgment, or failure. The world teaches us to hide our weaknesses, cover our flaws, and build walls to protect ourselves. But God's Kingdom operates on a different principle.

As I got older, I noticed a trend within my family to behave like tough nuts. I no longer co-sign to that lifestyle I'm afraid. God became a refuge for me, my solace. His Spirit held me through every breakdown, every mental shutdown, heartbreak, or betrayal. You name it, He was there!!!

When I got used to people disappearing from my life for one reason or another, God stayed with me. He had no expectations of me other than being his child whom He loves. The same is said and believed about you.

God heals in stages and with partnership. He can't and will not heal what we choose to ignore and avoid. My Pastor would often say "God can't deliver you from what you call a friend, only your enemy".

I struggled with depression for years. After God healed my broken heart, we had to deal with the wrath and self-hatred that was lying beneath. All those things were only possible through open and honest conversations and prayer.

"O Lord my God,
I cried to You for help, and You have healed me."
Psalm 30:2 AMP

You have done such a good job at being strong that everyone believes you are, including yourself. God will not heal what we choose to be quiet about, what we refuse to acknowledge and face. He speaks the language of tears and the whispers of heartaches. He's not afraid of your anger, frustration or delinquency. All He cares about is renewing His children and leading them well.

I get it. Life threw punches and you had no choice but to fight back. You had to be 'strong' for so long that it scares you to be 'weak' in front of anyone, even the one who made you. He's not asking for perfection. He's not asking for your vain attempts at being put together. He wants you—your tattered heart, wounded mind and broken spirit.

> *'Therefore, confess your sins to one another [your false steps, your offenses], and pray for one another, that you may be healed and restored. The heartfelt and persistent prayer of a righteous man (believer) can accomplish much [when put into action and made effective by God, it is dynamic and can have tremendous power]."*
> **James 5:16 AMP**

Vulnerability, when expressed in community, allows us to experience healing in ways that we cannot achieve on our own. It is in allowing ourselves to be seen and known by God and others that we begin the process of restoration.

It wasn't until I decided to be vulnerable that true healing began. God knew what was hurting me. He knows what is hurting you. He wants to heal you and restore your heart. The Lord is close to the broken-hearted, but He is also a gentleman. You must be willing to allow Him in. When He knocks upon the door of your heart, He isn't expecting it to be sparkly clean and without blemish. He isn't eagerly waiting to condemn you just because you don't have all your ducks in a row.

This is the key to deep intimacy with God. Just as we cannot fully experience a close relationship with anyone unless we allow ourselves to be open and honest, the same is true in our relationship with the Lord. When we come to Him with our weaknesses, fears, and pain, we invite Him into the depths of our hearts.

He knows we are just human. Humans who make mistakes; humans who do bad things sometimes, who break and don't want to be put together because we fear what could happen if someone sees who we really are.

Scared, lonely, mourning.

Our identity in Christ is deeply tied to our willingness to be vulnerable. We are not perfect, and we don't need to pretend to be. We are children of God, loved and accepted, not because of our perfection, but because of Christ's perfection. Embracing our vulnerability allows us to receive the love, grace, and acceptance God freely offers.

It's through this vulnerability, we discover the truth that God's power is made perfect in weakness—that His grace is enough, and that His love is unconditional. We are free to be real with Him, knowing that He sees us as we truly are and loves us anyway.

There is a profound beauty in vulnerability. It is not a weakness but a sacred space where God meets us in our brokenness, heals us, and transforms us. Through vulnerability, we experience intimacy, healing from our wounds, and a deeper connection with others. It is in our vulnerability that we discover the strength and power of God—and it is in our surrender that we fully embrace our identity in Christ.

The beauty of vulnerability lies in the truth that it is through our weaknesses that God's grace shines most brightly. When we allow ourselves to be seen, to be real, and to be known, we create space for God to do His most powerful work in and through us.

You are not alone. Though the nights seem to stretch on forever and your tears could refresh the ocean, you can be vulnerable and allow The Holy Spirit to show you just how renewing it can be.

You don't need to have it all figured out. You do not need to be good for Him to love you. He'd rather have an honest heart than a lying tongue. Take it as it comes. Lean into your community. Ask for help. I know it's hard, but you never know until you try. Life will come to test you, but God will forever be God.

You can do hard things. He has given you the ability to do hard things. There is beauty, joy and healing in your vulnerability.

Journal Prompts

1. What about your life have you hidden instead of being honest with God or others about?

2. What are you afraid people will see if you're fully known?

3. What would healing look like if you allowed God to meet you in your most vulnerable space?

Reflection

_____

_____

_____

_____

_____

_____

_____

_____

_____

Identity vs Reality

_____

_____

_____

_____

_____

_____

_____

_____

_____

_____

_____

_____

_____

_____

_____

_____

_____

_____

_____

_____

_____

_____

Chapter 6

Rejection is Redirection

"Rejection is Redirection"- Dr. Terri-Karelle Johnson

Rejection is one of the most painful experiences a person can go through, especially when it affects their sense of identity. It can feel like a personal blow to who a person is, leaving them questioning their worth and value. However, in the Kingdom of God, rejection is not the end of the story. Instead, it can be seen as redirection, God's way of guiding us to something better, more aligned with His purpose for our lives.

Rejection will have you stuck in situations and relationships that are sucking the life out of you, all because you want to be loved or seen while God desires you as you are, flaws and all. You don't need to pretend with Him.

Rejection often comes when we are seeking approval or validation from the wrong sources. Whether this is from people, jobs, relationships, or even ourselves, the world's standards of success and acceptance are often fickle and shallow. God's plan, however, is much deeper. His purpose for us is not defined by worldly approval, but by His divine calling.

"He came to that which was His own [that which belonged to Him, His world, His creation, His possession], and those who were His own [people, the Jewish nation] did not receive and welcome Him."
John 1:11 AMP

When we experience rejection, it's important to remember that God has a purpose behind it. Jesus Himself faced rejection, yet He knew it was part of His journey toward fulfilling His mission. Rejection, in this sense, can be a part of God's redirection, leading us away from the things that are not in His will and toward the path He has prepared for us.

Between late 2022 to mid 2023, I was employed at an organization that I thought was the best thing that had ever happened to me. However, the reality was not reflecting my delusions. I was working almost every day of the week, being paid below minimum wage, and doing jobs that probably should have been delegated to more than one person.

During my time at this establishment, it became painstakingly apparent just how deep rejection had embedded itself into my psyche. I did everything in my power to appease my superior, but I would often come up short on their expectations. This led me to falling into a deep season of depression. The joy I once felt was slowly becoming despair and rage. Let's just say it wasn't one of my finest hours.

My family and friends kept telling me to leave and explained that it wasn't worth it, but I stayed because I didn't believe there would be any better than this. I was fresh out of college, never had an official job and got hired without an interview. Where else could that possibly happen?

That was one of the hardest decisions I've had to make. Do I give up 'good' right now for the possibility of 'great' tomorrow? What if there is no better? What if it gets worse?

I eventually left, more so out of obedience than willingness.

Several mind-altering things took place after that. Doors that were once opened kept closing. People who I cleaved to at the beginning of the year started to turn away from me.

All the plans I thought would come through for me, failed. Rejection was my bread and butter. Amidst all of that, the Holy Spirit believed that was the best time to uncover past trauma.

Don't we just love when He does that?

It was painful to remember, but necessary. For context, my mom conceived me when she was 18 and tried to abort me. I remember her explaining that when she found out, she was filled with fear.

Impregnated by a man she hated, yet found comfort in his arms. How on earth was she going to tell my grandmother? To her, the most logical response would be to get rid of it before anyone found out.

Having no access to the safer medical way she turned her sights to 'home remedies'. When none of those options seemed to have worked and her depression grew, she believed her only available option was to end her life.

She explained that as she was about to go through with it, something compelled her not to. Breaking down in tears she decided to have me at 19.

At the time I felt so heartbroken. My mom didn't want me. No kid wants to hear that.

I kept asking God why He would remind me of something like that now. How can I write about 'Overcoming Rejection' when even from conception I was unwanted?

"Before I formed you in the womb I knew you [and approved of you as My chosen instrument], And before you were born I consecrated you [to Myself as My own]; I have appointed you as a prophet to the nations."
Jeremiah 1:5 AMP

God knew me. He knew that one day I'd go through these hurdles. He knew I'd find out about it and how it would break me. He also knew that one day He would use that very story to heal others.

Rejection can be painful, but it often forces us to grow in ways we might not grow otherwise. Rejection shaped my life for years. Every choice I made, the bonds I formed, came from the singular thought of "I want to be worthy of being loved and kept."

When we are rejected, we are given the opportunity to face our fears, doubts, and insecurities, and bring them before God. It can strip away the false identities we've constructed for ourselves—identities based on external validation, so that we can discover who we truly are in Christ.

God uses rejection to refine us. He allows us to go through experiences that shape and mold us into the people He has called us to be. Just as gold is refined by fire, our character and faith are often strengthened through the rejection we face.

"And we know [with great confidence] that God [who is deeply concerned about us] causes all things to work together [as a plan] for good for those who love God, to those who are called according to His plan and purpose.'
Romans 8:28 AMP

Sometimes, rejection is simply God's way of closing a door that was never meant for us. Whether it's a job, a relationship, or a dream that we hold on to tightly, God in His wisdom knows what's best for us. When we face rejection, it's essential to trust that He is leading us in the right direction. The door that closes may seem devastating, but it may be keeping us from a path that would ultimately be harmful or unfulfilling.

Even in rejection, God's hand is at work, redirecting us toward His perfect plan. What seems like a loss in the moment can often be a blessing in disguise as we look back and see how God was guiding us all along.

Rejection, when seen through the lens of God's love and sovereignty, becomes a powerful tool for redirection. It is not something to be feared, but something to be embraced. Our identity in Christ gives us the freedom to face rejection without being defined by it. Instead of seeing rejection as a failure, we can view it as an opportunity to be redirected by God toward something greater, surpassing our very imaginations.

As we walk through life's rejections, we can trust that God is working behind the scenes, leading us closer to His will and purpose. His ways are higher than ours, and His plans are always for our good. In Christ, rejection is never the final word, redemption is.

Journal Prompts

1. Who or what rejected you that left a scar on your identity?

2. What did that rejection teach you about yourself and is it the truth or is it a lie?

3. How is God using what seemed like rejection as divine redirection?

Reflection

_____

_____

_____

_____

_____

_____

_____

_____

_____

_____

Chapter 7

Change Your Default: The Power of the Process

P astor Trudy, one of the pastors at my church, once preached a sermon called 'Changing Your Default'. It's on YouTube. If you're curious you may view it.

I like to believe that it was one of those sermons that God used to infiltrate my 'protective' shell. At the time, I was going to church regularly, something I always wanted to do but there wasn't much of a change happening in me. I felt and acted the same as I had before, until that sermon.

Growth, healing, and transformation do not happen overnight. The journey to reclaiming your identity in Christ is a process, one that requires patience, faith, and perseverance. Though we may desire instant change, God often uses the process to refine us, strengthen us, and prepare us for His purpose.

Many of us resist the process because it feels uncomfortable. We want immediate breakthroughs, but God is more concerned with our development than our speed. Just as gold is purified through fire, our identity is refined through trials, challenges, and seasons of waiting.

CHANGE YOUR DEFAULT

What does that even mean? The simple definition is *'to fail to fulfil a contract, agreement, or duty'*. Before the world there was a version of you that God knitted into your mother's womb, with a plan, a purpose and a potential.

After birth, you grew and became influenced by your environment. This caused you to develop certain traits, coping and defence mechanisms, behaviours, etc. These influences become your default. They are how you deal with life's obstacles and rewards. These default responses may lead to feelings of inadequacy, rejection, and doubt about who you are in Christ.

For me, that was over-sexualizing myself and placing my worth in people's opinions instead of who Jesus said I am. Given, I had no clue what that entailed, I was of the belief that there was just too much that I had done to be 'cleaned up'. I thought I wasted too much of God's time trying to fix me. How was I going to make up for all that lost time?

In Ephesians 4:22-24, Paul urges believers to put off the old self, which is corrupted by deceitful desires, and put on the new self, created to be like God in true righteousness and holiness. Changing your default begins with recognizing what the old, false default looks like in your life.

If you've ever experienced rejection in the past, your default may be to assume that people will always abandon you, and you may struggle with feelings of unworthiness. God knows I have. Alternatively, if you grew up with a performance-based mentality, you may default to thinking that your worth is tied to what you do rather than who you are in Christ. These defaults are often lies that the enemy uses to keep us from living in the fullness of God's truth about us.

"Do not remember the former things or ponder the things of the past. Listen carefully, I am about to do a new thing, Now it will spring forth; Will you not

be aware of it? I will even put a road in the
wilderness, Rivers in the desert."
Isaiah 43:18-19 AMP

I have learnt that God is a redeemer. He told me to forget the past. It has already gone but what He had in store for me would far surpass all my dreams.

To change our default, we must begin the process of renewing our minds daily. The world's way of thinking is often rooted in fear, self-reliance, and competition. God's way of thinking, however, is rooted in love, grace, and trust in His provision. Changing your default means rejecting the old, worldly mindset and embracing the new mindset that comes from being rooted in Christ.

To do this, spend time in God's Word daily. The Scriptures remind us of our identity in Christ. When we meditate on God's promises, we begin to align our thoughts and attitudes with His truth rather than the lies the enemy has used to shape our old defaults.

There are key lessons God taught me in this process:

1. ***Dependence on God***: When we rely on our own strength, we often fail. God uses the

process to teach us dependence on Him (Proverbs 3:5-6).

2. ***Trusting His Timing***: God's timing is perfect. Even when we feel delayed, He is never late. His process is designed to prepare us for what is to come (Ecclesiastes 3:1).

3. ***Developing Character***: The process builds perseverance, patience, and humility. God is more interested in who we are becoming than in where we are going (Romans 5:3-4).

In fully accepting that truth, I needed to be willing to allow the Holy Spirit to take the reins, aiding in the process of returning me to factory settings. One of the joys of this kingdom life is that God has a habit of using everything for our good; nothing we go through is wasted.

"But all these things are from God, who reconciled us to Himself through Christ [making us acceptable to Him] and gave us the ministry of reconciliation [so that by our example we might bring others to Him], that is, that God was in Christ reconciling the world to Himself, not counting people's sins against them [but cancelling them]. And He has committed to us the message of reconciliation [that is, restoration to favour with God]."
2 Corinthians 5:18-19 AMP

The first step in changing your default is understanding your new identity in Christ. When you accept Christ you are a new creation, and your old identity—shaped by sin, insecurity, and shame is replaced with a new identity rooted in Christ's love and sacrifice.

When we choose to align with God a shift takes place. More often than not, you don't know it happens until the things you once took great joy in no longer entice you. There will be many moments when you want to respond out of your old mechanisms but remember you are transformed and that any man once he is in Christ is a new creature, the old things have passed.

"I am convinced and confident of this very thing, that He who has begun a good work in you will [continue to] perfect and complete it until the day of Christ Jesus [the time of His return]."
Philippians 1:6 AMP

Your identity is defined by who God says you are, not by your past mistakes, failures, or limitations. You are chosen, loved, forgiven, and called to a higher purpose.

The more you understand and meditate on this truth, the more your "default" will begin to shift. Instead of automatically thinking, "I'm not enough," or "I'm worthless," you start defaulting to the truth that you are deeply loved by God, and you have been given a purpose in His Kingdom.

When we truly accept Jesus into our hearts, through the help of the Holy Spirit we are as the scripture says brought back to 'Himself'. We no longer see ourselves or others through the eyes of trauma and hurt but instead as the beloved people He died on the cross to save.

Changing your default is a process that takes time. It's not something that happens overnight, and there will be setbacks along the way. But the key is to keep moving forward in grace and patience, trusting that God is at work in you. You may stumble or fall, but don't let that discourage you. Remember, your identity in Christ is secure, and He is transforming you day by day. Trust the process and rely on His grace to continue the work He has started with you.

The truth is the transition between leaving the world and following Jesus is hard. It is testing and at times taxing. Our main assurance and comfort is that we no longer have to do life alone.

Who God created you to be can only be stalled by your own decisions. The journey of discovering Christ is a process. Be reminded that though Jesus did the hard part of bridging the gap you still have a role to play in your timely deliverance. He has made every provision for your healing but the thing about provisions is that they still need to be harvested and accessed.

I remember always being burdened by my circumstances, the people around me. Today, I'm joyful that my life wasn't always filled with sunshine and rainbows because it gave God the perfect gateway to stir up and clean up my life. I'm zealous because He gave me a new life. Only the Holy Spirit can do a new thing within you.

"You will never understand the true potential within you without seeking the One who made you."

Changing your default is about intentionally aligning your thoughts, beliefs, and actions with the truth of who you are in Christ. It involves renewing your mind with His Word, rejecting lies, and choosing to live out the reality of your new identity.

By the power of the Holy Spirit, you can change the way you think, feel, and behave, and start reflecting the person God has created you to be. As you make this shift, you will experience greater freedom, peace, and fulfilment, knowing that your identity is secure in Christ and that you are living in alignment with His truth and purpose for your life.

My encouragement to you is that you have a choice. You have been gifted with free will. This means you can choose whether to remain complacent or be compelled to chase after what is yours—salvation and purpose.

Change your default, enter into your identity, and be reminded that you stand upon solid rock, Christ the firm foundation.

Journal Prompts

1. What "default" thoughts, behaviours, or survival mechanisms are no longer serving your purpose?

2. In what areas have you been resisting the process of transformation?

3. Ask God: *"What stronghold do You want to replace with truth today?"*

Reflection

_____

_____

_____

_____

_____

_____

_____

_____

Chapter 8

The Necessity of Purity While Finding Your Identity in Christ

Growing up I had a skewed idea of what purity was. What being pure meant. I never understood how distorted that view was until I began my journey with Christ.

As a child, I was molested by two family friends. After a while, I began to register it as a form of love because that's the nonsense they fed me, and as someone who, at that time, didn't have the best representation or understanding of what healthy love looked like, I fell for it.

This led to years of hypersexual behaviours. I developed a horrible porn addiction and masturbation was my favourite pastime. I sexualized myself for any hot-blooded male that gave me an ounce of attention. My mood swung on the pendulum of his responses.

Purity and identity are deeply connected. The enemy seeks to distort our perception of who we are by introducing distractions, temptations, and lies. If we allow impurity whether through sin, toxic influences, or false beliefs to take root, it can cloud our understanding of our true identity in Christ.

I read a quote somewhere that said, *"Sin feels like freedom until you try to quit."* Truer words have never been spoken. The more I took my walk with Christ seriously the more I began to see the impact of how years of sexual exposure had perverted my thought processes.

Without thinking, I would become romantically attracted to anyone who gave me any signs of care or affection that I wasn't used to. I didn't understand how to be loved platonically so if you cared for me in a certain way, I was smitten.

I couldn't properly engage in conversations with people without subconsciously sexualising them, entertaining 'situationships' because if they were attracted to me who cares what we were. I had no regard for myself and in turn saw others the same.

Food is for the stomach and the stomach for food, but God will do away with both of them. The body is not intended for sexual immorality, but for the Lord, and the Lord is for the body [to save, sanctify, and raise it again because of the sacrifice of the cross].
1 Corinthians 6:13 AMP

Finding your identity in Christ is a process of peeling away lies and stepping into truth. It's about discovering who God says you are, and learning to walk in that identity with confidence, freedom, and peace. Purity plays a crucial role in this journey.

God offers us grace and a path to purification. When we fall, we must repent, seek His forgiveness, and allow Him to cleanse us. Purity is a daily commitment to choosing God above all else. As we allow Him to refine us, we grow in our understanding of who we truly are in Christ.

Not because God requires perfection, but because purity clears the way for clarity. When your heart and soul are pure you can hear His voice more clearly. You begin to see yourself the way He does.

I must also emphasize that purity isn't just attributed to sexual immorality, it's any harmful behaviour that can distort our perception of self. Things that you know deep down are killing you spiritually but they're all you've known for so long.

Trying to let go of years of using the same medicine to treat the same wounds, you become numb to the possibility of sobriety. It becomes second nature. To reach for an explicit site, a glass, a blunt. Whatever gives the quickest relief with the least amount of effort and brain power.

It doesn't help that, regrettably, these topics are still treated as taboo in some parts of the body of Christ. It makes you feel dirty, guilty, and unworthy. If you can't open up about it, how can you no longer be bound by it?

"Watch over your heart with all diligence,
For from it flows the springs of life."
Proverbs 4:23 AMP

Finding your identity in Christ requires a heart that is open and surrendered. As we pursue purity, we unlock the fullness of our identity and purpose, gaining the ability to walk in the freedom and confidence that comes from knowing who we are in Him.

When we have no understanding of who we are and what we carry it's easy to be deceived by the false comfort that things can bring. I can't tell you the countless relationships I've entertained that I had no business being in but stayed because 'who else will love me like them?'

Deceit is such a slippery fellow. It poses as everything you want but nothing that actually benefits you. Everything we do flows from our hearts. A heart contaminated by sin or deception struggles to see itself through God's eyes. Protecting our hearts from negative influences allows us to fully embrace our identity as children of God.

Deceivers never approach authority; they always seek a backdoor to sneak through.

"Therefore I urge you, brothers and sisters, by the mercies of God, to present your bodies [dedicating all of yourselves, set apart] as a living sacrifice, holy and well-pleasing to God, which is your rational (logical, intelligent) act of worship."
Romans 12:1-2 AMP

Some time ago this scripture became etched upon my heart. It's not like I didn't know it before, but now it had a meaning deeper than just ink on paper. That's one of the joys of the Bible; it's the **living** word.

There's always something that in one season you glanced over but in the next it is what's carrying you through.

To be a living sacrifice means dying daily. EVERY. SINGLE. DAY! Taking up your cross even when you'd rather be on a beach with a Piña Colada. Purity holds a special place in discovering your identity in Christ because it involves setting your heart and mind on things that honour God. Purity is not about perfection but about a heart that seeks God above all else.

Living a life of purity is about aligning your actions and thoughts with God's will; making choices that reflect your commitment to Him and His teachings. As you pursue purity, you become more attuned to God's presence and His purpose for your life.

"Blessed [anticipating God's presence, spiritually mature] are the pure in heart [those with integrity, moral courage, and godly character], for they will see God."
Matthew 5:8 AMP

Purity is not just about what we avoid but about what we gain. When we live pure lives, we experience greater spiritual clarity, deeper intimacy with God, and a stronger understanding of who we are in Him. A pure heart allows us to see God's plans and purpose for our lives more clearly.

I spent most of my adolescence enraptured by porn; it became a comfort, something familiar when I was uncertain because it was always the same. What I didn't see was how subconsciously it made me more withdrawn, anxious—that post-nut clarity was no joke.

As I continued to fix my eyes on Jesus, the less I wanted to engage in it, but the harder the urges felt. I was trying to unravel years of attachment. I'm not saying God couldn't have instantly delivered me. I've heard testimonies of Him doing just that but I remember my Pastor telling me that "some things God delivers us from, some things He delivers us out of and some things He delivers us through".

It became a pain in the butt. I wanted to be holy. My mind and spirit were telling me no, but good Lord my body! Sheesh!

When sheer will power wasn't working, I had to create boundaries for myself.

I was an avid romance reader. I stopped reading those novels, switched to non-fiction and self-help. I disabled and hid Google Chrome off my phone and used normal Google (yes, there's a difference). I love anime and manga, and even those I had to schedule a day a week to catch up on but not get consumed by. I had a few friends who knew the struggle and kept me accountable. Lastly, I slept with my Bible on my bed, just as an extra reminder to keep my thoughts PG-13.

I know that may sound like I'm overdoing it but when you love someone it doesn't matter the lengths you go just to make them happy. Heck, people are doing way more for someone who won't even text back.

Yes, it may sound foolish to some, but God is not a stranger to using foolish things to confound the wise. Guard your heart. If you slip, repent quickly. Ask Him to walk with you through this. Sobriety in any capacity is a rough journey but it's necessary, nonetheless.

At its core, purity is about identity. It's about living in a way that reflects who you already are in Christ: a new creation, a royal priesthood, a child of the

King, and when you live out of that truth, the world begins to see Him in you.

Here's some extra pointers for why purity matters to your identity:

1. ***Purity Reflects Whose You Are*** - You belong to a holy God. Purity isn't about earning His love, it's a response to it. It shows that you recognize your worth and that you've been bought with a price (1 Corinthians 6:19–20).

2. ***Purity Protects Your Purpose*** - God has a unique calling on your life. Living pure in heart, mind, and body keeps your spiritual ears open and your path uncluttered. It helps you discern His voice and direction with clarity.

3. ***Purity Restores and Redeems*** - Even if you've stumbled in the past, your purity can be reclaimed. In Christ, there's no condemnation (Romans 8:1). He doesn't just forgive, He restores. Your story, no matter how broken, becomes a testimony of grace and redemption.

4. ***Purity Mirrors Jesus' Love*** - To be pure is to love as Jesus loves with integrity, with sacrifice, and with no hidden motives. It teaches you to see others as God sees them: worthy, valuable, and sacred.

Journal Prompts

1. What distractions, compromises, or idols have made it hard to hear God clearly?

2. How has impurity (in mind, motive, or lifestyle) distorted your perception of who you are in Christ?

3. What would it look like if you pursued purity, not out of fear, but as a response to God's love?

Reflection

_____

_____

_____

_____

_____

_____

_____

_____

Identity vs Reality

Chapter 9

From Servanthood to Sonship

"But to as many as did receive and welcome Him, He gave the right [the authority, the privilege] to become children of God, that is, to those who believe in (adhere to, trust in, and rely on) His name"
John 1:12 AMP

Each chapter has been a journey that the Lord has revealed to me during different seasons. This one was single-handedly the hardest lesson for me to learn. The process of moving from the mind of a servant to that of a son (daughter) took more from me than I thought it could.

I like helping in whatever way I can. I didn't grow up with money, so I tried to replace that with being present. I enjoy watching people's faces light up or their shoulders sag in relief because they have a little help. It encouraged me. I didn't think that was a bad thing. It's not. However, the issue began when I felt more comfort being a servant than a son.

A servant works for approval, while a son operates from approval. A servant is driven by duty, but a son is motivated by love. Jesus did not come just to make us workers in the Kingdom; He came to restore our relationship with the Father and establish us as His children.

I did not have the best example of parenting growing up. My family loved me the way they knew how and the way they were, but everyone needs different things. The culture was 'if you want something you have to work for it" (I still believe in that). The downside, which I've realised, is that I applied that to every aspect of my life.

I worked for everything, pushed myself beyond my limits because I wanted to prove that I am worthy of the love I so badly craved. I believed that if I worked hard enough someone would see me and give me a morsel of affirmation. This mindset got me in both beautiful and painful situations.

"For you have not received a spirit of slavery leading again to fear [of God's judgment], but you have received the Spirit of adoption as sons [the

*Spirit producing sonship] by which we [joyfully]
cry, "Abba! Father!".*
Romans 8:15 AMP

I didn't grow up with my father. The closest representation to a father figure I had was my uncle, who gave me bag juice as a baby because he didn't have the capabilities to produce milk. Love that guy. But even so, he himself was a child (we're 10 years apart). The other male that I had known died the day before I turned 11.

Not sure if you can tell, but the concept of a father was very foreign to me. The idea of being loved intentionally and unconditionally was greatly far-fetched.

Many of us unknowingly operate under an orphan spirit, feeling distant from God, unworthy of His love, and constantly trying to prove our value. This mindset leads to fear, insecurity, and strife.

I hadn't realized how deeply rooted this was until I finally found a church home. These people were so nice and friendly. I never expected it. It wasn't something I was used to. I mean, I could have been a mad person off the street, and they were hugging me. Crazy!

After some time, I just became woven into their membership. I served everywhere I could, and it made me so happy. Because it meant they were seeing me, it meant I was included, even if I wasn't wanted, I was needed. Or so I thought.

"It is vain for you to rise early, to retire late, to eat the bread of anxious labors. For He gives [blessings] to His beloved even in his sleep."
Psalm 127:2 AMP

Sleep and I have a love-hate relationship. If I need to get something done, I refuse to 'rest' until it's done, because I'd be too anxious. I had a habit of running myself ragged all in the name of showing up. Yes, I knew it was a problem. The Lord is working on my heart.

In September 2024, I was placed on a sabbatical and told to rest. It felt like they cursed a long line of expletives at me. I felt discarded and worthless because who was I, if not a servant?

That time of sabbatical felt like I was being torn. Why am I in a space and not doing anything when I can obviously be of assistance? Why am I watching my friends be involved in the things we did together but now I'm excluded? Was I that expendable? These questions plagued my mind.

Many believers struggle with understanding their position in God's Kingdom; living with a servant mentality striving to earn God's love, acceptance, and favour, rather than embracing their identity as sons and daughters of God. While servanthood has its place in our walk with Christ, God calls us to a deeper relationship, sonship.

I was angry, frustrated, and confused. After the time of kicking and screaming had passed the Lord began to deal with my heart. He showed me that I was using service as an escape from worship. It's hard to fill an ever-moving cup. What's the point of being busy when you're empty?

"See what an incredible quality of love the Father has shown to us, that we would [be permitted to] be named and called and counted the children of God! And so we are! For this reason the world does not know us, because it did not know Him."
1 John 3:1 AMP

I recall one Friday night, walking to the pickup location to go to our youth meeting and just dwelling with the Holy Spirit. I was just thankful for the experiences I've had, and I was sharing with Him my need for a laptop. I knew I was to have faith, but I remembered saying "You've been more than kind to me Lord. I shouldn't ask for more." I remember a voice saying "You're my child. You're supposed to ask me for things"; to which I responded, "Just because I'm your child doesn't make me obligated to get things from you." The response was "You sound like an orphan".

I heard it like I'd heard my name and wept in that parking lot. Those were words I told myself all my life.

As sons/daughters, we have direct access to God, your Heavenly Father. We can approach Him boldly, knowing we are loved and accepted, not because of our works, but because of what Jesus did (Hebrews 4:16). We are no longer distant or separated but are brought near by the blood of Christ.

It then occurred to me that if I wasn't placed on a sabbatical—not distracting myself with service and being forced to fix my eyes on Jesus, I wouldn't have received this revelation. Rest has a way of resetting our priorities.

Being a son of God means embracing your identity as a beloved child of God, fully accepted, loved, cared for and empowered by Him. It's a transformative relationship that goes beyond mere belief or servitude; sonship involves an intimate connection with God as our Father.

It changes everything about our prayers, our confidence, and our purpose. When we understand that we are heirs with Christ, we no longer live as slaves to fear and performance. Instead, we walk in the power and authority given to us as children of the King.

Learn to rest in the finished work of the cross. God is calling you to move beyond servanthood and embrace your true identity as His child.

"You don't need to be perfect, to be accepted."

To transition from servanthood to sonship, we must:

- *Recognize God as our Father* – Understanding that God is not just our Lord but our loving Father transforms how we relate to Him (Galatians 4:6-7).

- ***Rest in His Love*** – We do not have to earn His love; we already have it. When we embrace His unconditional love, we walk in confidence and freedom (1 John 3:1).

- ***Operate from Inheritance, Not Striving*** – Sons and daughters receive an inheritance; they do not have to work for their place in the family. Ephesians 1:11 reminds us that in Christ, we have obtained an inheritance.

Journal Prompts

1. Have you been relating to God as a servant trying to earn His approval or as a son/daughter resting in His love?

2. Where have you felt you needed to "perform" to be accepted?

3. What does it mean to you personally to be an heir, not just a helper?

Reflection

_____

_____

_____

_____

_____

_____

_____

_____

_____

_____

Identity vs Reality

Chapter 10

Obedience - The Greatest Sacrifice

Jesus replied to him, "You do not realize now what I am doing, but you will [fully] understand it later."
John 13:7

I've had many experiences with the Lord. The older I get the more I understand Paul when he says "To live is Christ but to die is great gain,"(**Philippians 1:21**) and David's declaration that "I was young and now I'm old; yet I have never seen the righteous forsaken, nor their seed begging bread."(**Psalm 37:25**)

Nearing the end of 2023, I heard the Holy Spirit telling me He was moving my family, but I wouldn't be going with them.

People of the Most High God.

I convinced myself for weeks that I was hearing things, and the Lord in His infinite kindness sent multiple people to affirm the very thing He had told me. Eventually, I came to terms with it in secret.

At the time, I was working in a nice job that paid decently, so I thought "Ok God, this looks like it can work, if I save enough and play my cards right, I can definitely move out." I lost the job. Yet, I had peace about the decision. That following Friday while serving at Woman Ignite Success Summit (WISS), my aunt informed me we had been evicted and had a month to relocate.

Now, I don't know about you, but I was ready to lose my marbles. Remember, He told and affirmed that we were moving but at no point did I expect this turn of events. I was told to withhold the information for a time just to keep it between Him and I. Eventually, I got the release to tell my family. Not the full scope of why but just that I wasn't going with them.

Slowly, but surely, the days went by. I did what He told me to do, informed who He instructed me to, kept quiet, kept serving. Never in life did I think I could have gone through something like that. My family had already found a new home, and I was still out of a job, no potential leads to a home—just living off faith, trust and a batch of pixie dust.

I remember the Sunday which would have marked almost a week before it was time to go. I still had nothing, and I crashed out in my church bathroom. It was as if the reality of the situation finally struck me. Did I mishear Him? Should I just move with my family? Maybe this is some form of punishment, and I was in disobedience? Doubt flooded my thoughts.

At the time, I was doing social media at church as I've mentioned before. That particular Sunday, I reluctantly served but did it because I had to trust the word He gave me. I chose obedience and submission. I felt a pull for me to go to the altar when my pastor made an altar call. Please note, it's not something that was done every Sunday, so I chalked it up to my soul being desperate for some answer or relief.

Wouldn't you know it, he did an altar call, and it floored me. Literally, it was the first time in my life, walking with Christ that I was flat faced weeping on the ground—"Whatever you say My Lord".

In less than a week, I got what I called the job of my dreams—working in media and production, and somewhere to live, in an area that baby Glacia would have never dreamed she could reside in.

So much sprung from that time, it grew my faith to the point where no one had to tell me about my God. I was told I wouldn't survive on my own and in truth deep down I thought the same, but as it turns out I was never alone. Though there were moments of silence, He never left me.

When you obey God, even in the secret place you affirm your true self: not a rejected, striving orphan, but a crowned son or daughter of the King. Rejection says, "Prove your worth." God says, "Walk in what I've already said".

When God asked Abraham to offer Isaac, it was a test, not of sacrifice, but of trust. God never intended for Isaac to die, though I doubt Abraham was privy to that knowledge. Yet, He wanted Abraham to trust Him enough to surrender his own understanding. That is obedience—trusting when you don't see the outcome and walking even when the road feels uncertain.

But if God is calling you deeper, you can trust that He has more for you, not just more to do, but more to become. Deep calleth unto deep (**Psalm 42:7**).

Since that leap, I have undergone pruning, been stripped down, daily dying to my flesh, dealing with matters I believed I was over but just distracted myself from. I've wept more tears than I thought I had in my body. I felt like Abraham on some days— told to leave his family to a land God would show him (**Gen 12:1-3**). On others I was like David, "How Long o Lord?" (**Psalm 13**) or "Who Am I, O Lord, that You have brought me this far.?"(**2 Sam 7 18-22**) —because it just felt like I was hidden from the world.

In every shift, turn and break, I received a deeper revelation of God and who He was calling me to be. Obedience doesn't always look impressive. Sometimes it means stepping away from the crowd, saying "no" to something good, or letting go of something you've always done in order to follow the fresh whisper of His Spirit.

WHEN OBEDIENCE COSTS YOU EVERYTHING

There's a kind of obedience that feels easy when it aligns with our comfort, when it's applauded by others, when it doesn't cost us anything meaningful. But there's another kind of obedience, the kind Jesus demonstrated that demands our will, our reputation, our very lives. It is this kind of obedience that heaven calls *the greatest sacrifice.*

If there's one thing I took from this 'isolation period', it is that obedience will cost you everything. Even the things you didn't think would have been a sacrifice. The bridge between rejection and identity involves a series of surrendering.

Jesus didn't just give something. He gave everything, through obedience and in doing so, He revealed a powerful truth: real obedience is not separate from sacrifice, *it is the highest form of it.*

Let this truth sink in: **Obedience flows from identity, not insecurity. Every act of obedience is an act of identity.**

OBEDIENCE IS AN ALTAR OF THE HEART

I remember one prayer meeting I was praying and found myself saying "I will lay my life at the altar of your feet, Lord. Burn me beautiful and burn me lovely". Please tell me I'm not the only one who has those moments after prayer where you want to retract the words that left your mouth.

Sacrifice in the Old Testament often meant giving something external: a lamb, an offering, a tithe. But in the New Covenant, sacrifice has moved inward. God is no longer looking for dead animals. He's looking for living altars.

When we think of overcoming rejection and reclaiming our crown, it's easy to picture strength, authority, and visibility. But before Jesus wore a crown of glory, He bore a crown of thorns. He was rejected, mocked, abandoned. His path to exaltation was paved with obedience. So, it must be for us.

And the greatest altar is the heart that says: "Not my will, but Thy will be done. Whatever You Say, My Lord."

That's obedience. Not blind submission, but trust-filled surrender. It is a declaration that God's way is better, even when it's hard; *especially when it's hard.*

True obedience is not about obligation; it's about relationship. It is saying, "I trust the One who calls me, even when I don't fully understand the path". In a world that tells us to assert our independence, obedience seems weak. But in the Kingdom, it is the foundation of royalty.

One of rejection's most subtle fruits is the desire for control. When you've been hurt, abandoned, or overlooked, your natural response is to protect yourself to make sure it never happens again. So, you take control of your life, your plans, even your faith.

But God cannot reign where we refuse to surrender. Sometimes obedience will cost you your pride. Sometimes it will cost you your plan. Sometimes it will cost you your visibility, your comfort, even relationships. But obedience will never cost you your identity. In fact, it is obedience that reveals it.

"Although He was a Son [who had never been disobedient to the Father], He learned [active, special] obedience through what He suffered."
Hebrews 5:8 AMP

Jesus, though perfect, was still formed by obedience.

What a mystery. Jesus learned obedience. This is not because He was rebellious, but because obedience is proven in pressure. He obeyed the Father unto death, and through that obedience, He reconciled the rejected. He opened the door for us to return not just to God's purpose, but to His presence.

Your obedience matters—more than your gifting, more than your visibility, more than your background or pain. Your obedience is what God uses to write redemption stories.

OBEDIENCE AS THE PATH TO ROYALTY

Reclaiming your crown isn't about demanding a throne. It's about submitting to the King. Though a prince or princess has access to be in the throne room and by blood, inherit the riches of their kingdom, they are not exempted from the ruling of their Monarch, though they are family.

It's about saying yes when it's costly, when it's lonely, when no one else understands.
God is not looking for the most qualified, but the most obedient.

David wasn't chosen because he was the strongest or most popular. He was chosen because he had a heart after God, a heart that obeyed, repented, and surrendered.

And here's the truth: **You don't get to wear the crown without first embracing the cross.**

Obedience is where you lay down your rights and take up His righteousness. It's where you surrender your script and let God write His story through your life. In the Kingdom of God, obedience isn't a weakness, it's power. It is the pathway from rejection to royalty, from fear to faith, from survival to sonship. You are not what others say you are. You are who God says you are and He's calling you to walk like it.

Obedience is not the absence of sacrifice. It is, in fact, the greatest one.

PRACTICAL STEPS TO WALK IN OBEDIENCE

- *Start with the small yes*: Obedience doesn't always begin with a big life-altering decision. It often starts with the quiet whisper: "Forgive," "Call them," "Be still," "Trust Me." "Apologize"

- *Get comfortable with not being understood:* Obedience might make you look foolish for a season. But don't trade obedience for approval.
- *Measure success by faithfulness, not outcome*: What God calls you to do may not look "successful" to the world. If He said it, that's enough.
- *Keep your heart tender*: Obedience is sustained not by willpower, but by love. Stay in communion with God. Keep your heart close to His voice.

Prayer

Father, I thank You for modelling perfect obedience through Jesus. Help me to trust You with every step, even when it costs me comfort or control. Where rejection has closed my heart, open it again through the power of surrender. I don't want to just offer You my actions, I want to give You my heart. Teach me to obey as a child of the King, not out of fear, but out of love. In Jesus' name, Amen.

Journal Prompts

1. What has God asked you to surrender that you've been afraid to let go of?
2. Where has delayed obedience affected your identity journey?
3. What could be unlocked in your purpose if you obeyed God fully and trusted Him completely?
4. In what areas of your life have you substituted sacrifice for obedience?
5. Can you identify any choices motivated more by fear of rejection rather than trust in God's direction?
6. What is God calling you to be obedient to today, even if it doesn't "look impressive"?

Reflection

_____

_____

_____

_____

_____

_____

Chapter 11

Seek First The Kingdom: It Takes a Village

Your Identity lives where your roots are.

The phrase "it takes a village" is often used to describe a combined effort needed to raise a child, but it holds much deeper significance when it comes to our identity in Christ. No one is meant to walk the journey of faith alone.

God designed the Church, the body of believers, to be a community that supports, encourages, and strengthens one another as we grow in our identity as sons and daughters of the King. Just as a child grows and thrives within a supportive community, so too do we, as children of God, need the village of believers to walk with us through the process of becoming who God has called us to be.

As I reflect upon the past couple years, all I can see is how vital godly community and partnerships are for growing in faith and how intentional God was about building that for me.

Like I said, this book almost didn't happen. I began believing that maybe I was mistaken, and God didn't really give me a message. Doubt and judgement clouded my mind. Thankfully, He placed me in the arms of some amazing people. Big Them Up Every Time!

I wasn't very good at making friends or keeping them. I would either be 'too much' or 'far too little' for their standards and as a past 'people pleaser' it hurt. Eventually, I became a loner. Though I often surrounded myself with people I was connected to, no one truly knew me. It wasn't the best state to be in, but it did what I needed it to. When I rededicated my life to God in 2020 one of my biggest prayers was that I wanted a community.

In March of 2021, I ended up joining the online aspect of a church in Ghana. God really used them to plant some much-needed seeds in me though I didn't stay there long. They helped ease my loneliness for a time. After my mom's passing that prayer became all

I could ask for because I wanted, no, needed someone to be there for me.

The latter part of that year I met a group of people who made me feel less alone. I thought this was God answering my prayer. May I just clarify that none of them were believers and though, on a journey back to the Lord, I was very lukewarm. Not one of my proudest moments.

There were a few people in particular that I held very dear to my heart. When you saw me, you saw them and vice versa. At the time I thought "this was it, they were my people". They became my worst heartbreak to date. Spent the majority of 2022 in depression and hatred because of what happened and even swore off any form of friendship and relationship after that.

Then came these three women I met while working a major event. We bonded while sitting at the altar of a church we were campaigning at. They 'healed' me. We were inseparable, especially one of them who took me as her little sister. She even later introduced me to what is now my home church. Man, I loved them. I thought 'what could possibly go wrong?"

Everything. Everything went wrong!

I lost that beautiful sisterhood due to misunderstandings and to the fact that once again I was 'inadequate'. I remember how angry I was after the situation unfolded. It was so bad that the very next day while explaining what happened to someone, I developed a fever and passed out.

I was so hurt and upset. I kept asking God "Why do you keep connecting me with people who always leave? Why can I never be enough for anyone?" I gave up. I truly believed I was meant to be alone and that needed to be enough for me.

As you can see, I have not had the best of luck where human relations were concerned.

"For just as in one [physical] body we have many parts, and these parts do not all have the same function or special use, so we, who are many, are [nevertheless just] one body in Christ, and individually [we are] parts one of another [mutually dependent on each other]."
Romans 12:4-5 AMP

We all belong to each other. Yet, I felt like I belonged nowhere. After that last situation I came to the decision that maybe it just needed to be me and Jesus for a while. It wasn't a choice I was particularly fond of, at that point what did I really have to lose?

I learned to fellowship with the Holy Spirit.

It was hard at first because sometimes I wanted to verbally hear a response to my worries or receive a hug when I needed one. Instead, I replaced them with reading the word more. Going to church and doing my best to pay attention. As this continued, I grew to love what I call 'Daddy Daughter Time'. The scriptures say that His sheep know His voice. The more intentional I was with knowing Him, the more He revealed Himself to me.

I started getting more involved in church by doing social media. Turns out I was good at it. Without realising it, I started positioning myself to serve anywhere I could. Looking back, I can see that the Lord was setting me up for some great opportunities. (If you have no idea what you're meant to do, seek Him, start serving and let Him lead.)

I started hanging out with my church family, correction, they kept flocking me with love. I wasn't used to it. They would ask me questions about me, give me random hugs, and say "It's great to see you

Glacii." To say I was perturbed was an understatement. However, I grew into their embrace.

"Two are better than one because they have a more satisfying return for their labour; for if either of them falls, the one will lift up his companion. But woe to him who is alone when he falls and does not have another to lift him up. Again, if two lie down together, then they keep warm; but how can one be warm alone? And though one can overpower him who is alone, two can resist him. A cord of three strands is not quickly broken."
Ecclesiastes 4:9-12 AMP

I can't tell you exactly when or how it started but before I knew it my heart became softer. My walls weren't so high anymore. I cried almost all the time, especially when I was happy. Without noticing, God surrounded me with love. A love I never expected and could have never predicted.

It wasn't just church either. The more I lost myself in Jesus the more He filled my space with people like Him; at work, in business, family, and friends. Not long after I had a support system far larger than I had capacity to comprehend. I didn't ask for it this time, the God who knows my needs supplied exactly that.

People who understood me and wanted nothing more than to see me be who God called me to be.

He gave me a village filled with family, mentors, leaders, etc. They played the most pivotal part in this journey. He healed me through His people. The very humanity I swore off. His sense of humour is superbly cracked if you ask me. Why am I telling you all this?—because I've come to the revelation.

REJECTION CAN ONLY BE REDEEMED BY RELATIONSHIP.

Often, it is from a form of relation that rejection is born. Whether you had a specific job in mind, but it didn't come to fruition; you were crushing on someone, and those feelings were not reciprocated; or family members that just don't seem to understand you the way you'd like.

One way or another you unconsciously bonded with an idea and because it didn't turn out in your favour, it altered something within you. Simultaneously, it takes a positive relationship in a similar case to redeem it.

My recommendation: Seek First the Kingdom of God and His righteousness. Watch all things be added unto you according to His will.

Rejection has a voice. It whispers, sometimes it screams—that you're not good enough, not wanted, not chosen. Over time, those words take root and form an identity shaped by pain. But Jesus offers a new voice, one that speaks life, purpose, and royal belonging.

This scripture has been tested and proven in my life especially this past season. Things started changing when I chose to sit at the feet of Jesus and be intentional about knowing Him. I stopped telling Him what I wanted and started asking what His plans are for me.

Was it easy? Definitely not. The closer I got to Him the more sinful and unworthy I felt and just like the Father He is, He'd always find the right time to pick me up and tell me how precious I was to Him and how much He saw my efforts; whether through His people, a dream or just quiet time in His presence.

He wants that with you. He wants to surround you with the right people. Those who will love and care for you without you having to compromise and hide. It truly takes a village to raise a child and whether we want to accept or not, we still have an inner child who wants nothing more than the love they were deprived of.

It's ok to be scared and hesitant to trust again especially after being hurt and betrayed, but it is possible. As we speak God is positioning your destiny helpers. I urge you not to make them wait too long.

Allow the Lord to be your friend just as He is your God. Allow Him to heal where it hurts so you can love more than you've ever loved before.

And let us not neglect our meeting together, as some people do, but encourage one another, especially now that the day of his return is drawing near.
Hebrews 10:25 AMP

Journal Prompts

1. What have you prioritized over the Kingdom of God in your search for identity?

2. Are you trying to walk in purpose alone? Who is in your God-assigned village?

3. How can you align your relationships, desires, and focus to seek the Kingdom first?

Reflection

_____

_____

_____

_____

_____

_____

_____

_____

_____

_____

Chapter 12

Be Fruitful and Multiply

"And God blessed them [granting them certain authority] and said to them, "Be fruitful, multiply, and fill the earth, and subjugate it [putting it under your power]; and rule over (dominate) the fish of the sea, the birds of the air, and every living thing that moves upon the earth."
Genesis 1:28 AMP

God gave humanity the instruction to be fruitful and multiply. It was part of God's original design for creation to flourish, spread, and reflect His glory. Being fruitful and multiplying is central to fulfilling God's purposes.

This goes beyond mere reproduction; it speaks to the idea of cultivating life in all areas. Being fruitful means living in a way that honours God, reflects His goodness, and brings His purpose into the world. Whether in relationships, work, ministry, or personal growth, we are called to bear good fruit that reflects our Creator's nature and brings others closer to Him.

When you walk in your God-given identity, fruit bears unconsciously. Like wine fresh out of the winepress, it just flows.

Our identity in Christ is foundational to our ability to be fruitful. As believers, we are no longer bound by the limitations of our old nature. We are now new creations in Christ (2 Corinthians 5:17). This new identity equips us to live in a way that produces fruit, spiritual fruit that glorifies God and benefits others. Our relationship with Jesus, who is the true vine, enables us to bear fruit that is in alignment with His will.

The fruit of the Spirit: love, joy, peace, long-suffering, kindness, goodness, faithfulness, gentleness, and self-control are the tangible expressions of the transformation that occurs when we embrace our identity in Christ. This fruit, not produced by our own efforts, are the result of the Holy Spirit working in and through us.

"I am the true Vine, and My Father is the vinedresser. Every branch in Me that does not bear fruit, He takes away; and every branch that

continues to bear fruit, He [repeatedly] prunes, so that it will bear more fruit [even richer and finer fruit]."
John 15:1-2 AMP

God is the master gardener. He trims away the vines that don't produce fruit while pruning the ones that do. As the ones connected to the true vine (Jesus) it's hard sometimes to remember that cutting and snipping are a part of being fruitful.

A quick Google search states "pruning is a key gardening practice that involves the selective removal of plant parts to enhance the health, shape, and feel. It requires knowledge of plant physiology, growth patterns, and a keen eye for detail."

Sometimes, God allows pruning in our lives to remove areas of unfruitfulness or selfishness. While this can be a painful process, it is necessary for us to grow and bear more fruit. The pruning process is not a punishment but an act of love, refining us to fulfil our purpose and live according to our identity in Christ.

Additionally, the enemy seeks to hinder our fruitfulness by planting seeds of doubt, fear, and discouragement. We must stand firm in our identity in Christ and resist the temptation to be distracted or disheartened.

How interesting is it that it requires knowledge of your biology (your internal makeup), your growth patterns—cycles that you go through—and a **keen eye** for detail. Who better to trim and snip than the one who knitted you in your mother's womb?

Every time you grow in knowledge you must grow in fruit.

In the crushing and pressing, it hurts. To be removed from the things you once found great comfort in, the things that you once found identity in; to have those parts of you stripped away, is daunting. The pain now makes you question and almost forsake the future promises.

Our identity in Christ allows us to see beyond the temporary and focus on the eternal impact of our lives. The fruit we bear and the disciples we make are part of the lasting legacy we leave in the Kingdom of God. In heaven, we will see the results of our faithfulness as we stand before God and witness the lives that have been transformed through His work in us.

Seasons change. An oak tree will remain an oak tree regardless of the change in climate. That's the stance I want us to have—to be so rooted in who Christ says we are, that no matter the storm, drought, leaves falling, new leaves growing, pruning, stripping, all of it—at the end of it all I want us to bear in and out of season.

"You have not chosen Me, but I have chosen you and I have appointed and placed and purposefully planted you, so that you would go and bear fruit and keep on bearing, and that your fruit will remain and be lasting, so that whatever you ask of the Father in My name [as My representative] He may give to you."
John 15:16 AMP

You are pruned to bloom. Bloom brightly. Bloom Spectacularly. Bloom Abundantly.

Take up space. Spread your roots in His word, endure the teething pains but don't lose sight of the vision He gave you. Dream big, believe for the more. Learn the fruits and produce accordingly.

You are gifted whether you believe it or not. What were the passions you had as a child? What were things that brought you the most joy and peace that rejection made you turn a blind eye to?

As Christians, we are called to multiply the Kingdom by leading others to Christ and helping them grow in their faith. This occurs not through human effort alone but through the empowerment of the Holy Spirit. Jesus promises that as we go and make disciples, He will be with us, guiding and strengthening us for the task.

Our identity in Christ includes the calling to be ambassadors of the Kingdom. As we bear fruit in our own lives, we are called to share the fruit of our transformation with others, inviting them to experience the same life-changing relationship with Jesus.

One of the funniest discoveries I've experienced on this journey of 'Reclaiming My Crown' is that I'm returning to baby Glacia. I wanted to be an author, a playwright, an actress, media and production practitioner—anything creative always fascinated me. But I was told I could never make a living from them—that I was 'doing too much' and needed to be more realistic.

Yet, here comes our Creator, resetting me to the time of childlike whimsy and big dreams. I am now in the creative space, thriving. Producing fruit, I didn't even know I had, but He did.

You are much. Be Much! Embrace every bit of 'muchness' that God gave you.

"Whatever you do [no matter what it is] in word or deed, do everything in the name of the Lord Jesus [and in dependence on Him], giving thanks to God the Father through Him."
Colossians 3:17 AMP

Fruitfulness is not limited to evangelism or ministry; it extends to all areas of life. We are called to bear fruit in our relationships, in our work, in our families, and in the way we engage with the world.

Abide in Christ. Live in constant relationship with Him: through prayer, studying His Word, and seeking His will. When we remain connected to Jesus, He empowers us to bear the fruit that He desires.

Abiding in Christ is not a one-time act but a continual choice to remain in Him daily. As we abide in His love and truth, the Holy Spirit works within us, producing fruit that reflects His character. Our identity in Christ enables us to rely on His strength, not our own, to live a life that is fruitful in every area.

Let us embrace our identity in Christ, knowing that we are called to be fruitful and multiply, both in our personal lives and in our witness to the world. As we live out this calling, we can trust that God will work in us and through us, bringing forth lasting fruit that reflects His love and power.

Journal Prompts

1. What fruit is your life bearing right now and does it reflect your identity in Christ?

2. Are you hiding your gifts out of fear, shame, or comparison?

3. Ask God: *"How do* You *want me to multiply what You've given me for Your glory?"*

Reflection

_____

_____

_____

_____

_____

_____

_____

_____

_____

_____

_____

Identity vs Reality

Chapter 13

Reclaim Your Crown

"Before I formed you in the womb, I knew you [and approved of you as My chosen instrument], And before you were born, I consecrated you [to Myself as My own]; I have appointed you as a prophet to the nations."
Jeremiah 1:5 AMP

"Therefore if anyone is in Christ [that is, grafted in, joined to Him by faith in Him as Savior], he is a new creature [reborn and renewed by the Holy Spirit]; the old things [the previous moral and spiritual condition] have passed away. Behold, new things have come [because spiritual awakening brings a new life]."
2 Corinthians 5:17 AMP

At the beginning of writing this book, I really wasn't sure if I had anything worth saying. A big question I kept asking the Lord was

"How does one reclaim a crown they didn't even know they had in the first place?"

Reality comes to break, shake and destroy us. Who we are and what we believe in is what keeps us rooted or moved. I encourage you to be rooted in Jesus. Grief will come, sadness will come, but the joy of the Lord is your strength.

You were called for a purpose, and purpose shouldn't die until the promise is fulfilled. Your birth wasn't a mistake as you may have previously believed. Your existence in time was premeditated and pre-planned before the foundation of the world was laid. Don't believe me? Check the scriptures. These are His words to us, and He has placed His word above His very name.

A name. Your name is not to be taken lightly. To leave a legacy you need to recognize the power of a name, and as a child, mine was always linked to anxiety or fear. Whether it was the stern way my mother said it as a sign I was tap dancing on her last nerve or how foreign it sounded out of my own mouth. I preferred to go by my pet name, Angel, for a great deal of my existence. It was easier to pretend to be someone else or to go by something else than accept the one I was born with.

Life feels a lot like that at times. It's just simpler to go by what others label you, than to correct or defend the truth.

I often remember encouraging people to use my nickname if they believed my birth name was too difficult. I rejected it before anyone else could have the chance to. I shrunk and downsized myself to fit into molds that were never meant for me. I often wonder if God frowned at the times I took on an identity which He didn't breathe life into.

It's comical now because the very same name I held such distaste for is now one that is spoken about and called upon often. The name that once was linked to my greatest heartbreaks, denials, and rejections; the name which I thought to be a burden, He linked to my liberation.

Reclaiming your crown is not just about words or declarations; it's about living out the fullness of your identity in Christ every day. It's about walking in confidence, peace, and victory, knowing that you are a child of the King—chosen and beloved.

Isn't it beautiful how the Holy Spirit will never address you as your current situation but instead by your prophetic destiny? Gideon was a prime example (**Judges 6:12**).

Sons receive an inheritance, and as a child of God, you are co-heir with Christ (Romans 8:17). This means that you have access to all the blessings and promises that belong to Jesus—eternal life, authority, and the fullness of God's provision.

Now faith is the assurance (title deed, confirmation) of things hoped for (divinely guaranteed), and the evidence of things not seen [the conviction of their reality faith comprehends as fact what cannot be experienced by the physical senses].
Hebrews 11:1 AMP

You must move from a space of knowing to believing. You can know a lot of things but still not believe them. A currency of the Kingdom is faith. In faith, I need you to know and believe that your true identity was knitted into your DNA long before anyone else had a say.

I say this because I want you to fight for your freedom. Don't give your mind up to the enemy that easily. Give him exactly, if not more than, what he's trying to bring to you. Contend for your identity, because I can tell you the enemy wants nothing more than for you to die with the very answer God placed in you for His people.

You are no longer alone. You have a vindicator. He is your shield and defence. You've come too far to allow the enemy any more leverage over you.

Prayer and worship are powerful tools in reclaiming your crown. They help to realign our hearts and minds with God's will and purpose for our lives. When we pray, we acknowledge our dependence on God and invite His will to be done in our lives. Worship, on the other hand, helps us focus on God's greatness and sovereignty, reminding us of our identity as His children.

Through prayer, we can declare God's promises over our lives, resist the enemy's lies, and claim victory in areas where we may have been defeated. Worship helps to restore our hearts to a place of gratitude, praise, and surrender, allowing us to reconnect with our royal identity in Christ.

You'll have bad days. You'll have great days. There will be days that you question if you even made the right decision by following Christ, but I can assure you that though weeping endures for a night, there really is joy in the morning (Psalm 30:5).

As you reclaim your crown, you step into the fullness of your calling and purpose. You begin to live in alignment with God's plans for your life, walking with the confidence that you are equipped to overcome any challenges that come your way. You no longer live as a victim or a slave to the enemy's lies but as a victorious child of God, crowned with His love, grace, and authority.

"But you are a chosen race, a royal priesthood, a consecrated nation, a [special] people for God's own possession, so that you may proclaim the excellencies [the wonderful deeds and virtues and perfections] of Him who called you out of darkness into His marvelous light."
1 Peter 2:9 AMP

As I reflect on these past seasons of my life — everything that happened from youth until now — all I can do is cry "Thank you, Abba." The girl who yearned for love was rescued by the definition of love. The depressed girl who thought her life meaningless was swept up in the arms of the Peacemaker himself. Rejected, the outcast, the orphan became a co-heir to Jesus and adopted by The God of the Universe. Hallelujah!

God took my wilderness and turned it into a garden. He rebuilt me in the seasons when I had no one else to count on, but His goodness sustained me.

He stripped me bare so I could help cover you.

When we reclaim our crown, we step into our role as kings and priests in God's Kingdom. As kings, we are called to rule with wisdom, justice, and righteousness—reflecting the reign of Jesus on earth. As priests, we are called to intercede for others, offering prayers and worship to God, and serving as ambassadors of reconciliation.

Our royal identity involves both authority and responsibility, both to reign and to serve. Living royally in God's Kingdom means understanding that our actions, words, and decisions carry weight and influence. We are not passive observers of life. We are active participants in bringing God's Kingdom to Earth.

"And if [we are His] children, [then we are His] heirs also: heirs of God and fellow heirs with Christ

[sharing His spiritual blessing and inheritance], if indeed we share in His suffering so that we may also share in His glory."
Romans 8:17 AMP

I implore you to stop taking everything from everyone, who has not been green-lighted to be in your space, as gospel. It is by their fruits that you will know them, and if the fruits are not of Christ why pick from the tree?

Reclaiming your crown is about taking back what has been stolen or neglected; the promises, power, and identity that are rightfully yours in Christ. When we take our place as sons and daughters of the King, we begin to walk in the fullness of His blessings and favour.

It also means embracing the inheritance that has been given to us. As co-heirs with Christ, we share in His inheritance, which includes both spiritual and earthly blessings. This inheritance gives us access to all the resources we need to fulfil our divine purpose.

The power of reclaiming your crown lies in the realization that you have been equipped with everything you need to live victoriously. You have been given power, love, wisdom, and authority through the Holy Spirit, and with this power, you can overcome any obstacle and fulfil the purpose for which you were created.

As I lay my heart out within each line and punctuation of this book, I hope that something spoke to you, even if it was only one word. I pray that you make the conscious decision to change your default from the world's experience and back to who God made you to be.

May this not make you continue to say, "One day it'll get better," but instead say, "Day one of being the one He knew" (Matthew 7:21-23). You were placed on this earth because God foresaw a problem and knew you would be the perfect solution. You can't operate in that without first knowing who and whose you are. Only the baker can tell you exactly how their signature cake was made, what occasion it is best suited for and why it is their most treasured creation.

Reclaiming your crown is an act of faith and determination. It is choosing to believe in the truth of who you are in Christ and stepping into the royal identity that has been granted to you as a son or daughter of the King. Through Christ, you have been given authority, purpose, and inheritance, and it's time to embrace and walk in the fullness of all that God has prepared for you.

As you reclaim your crown, remember that you are not alone. God, through the Holy Spirit, empowers you to live out your royal identity, and the victory is already yours. Stand firm, resist the enemy, and walk confidently in the authority that has been given to you as a beloved child of God.

Journal Prompts

1. What would it look like for you to fully reclaim your crown: emotionally, spiritually, relationally?

2. What must die in you so that the true identity in Christ can rise?

3. Write a declaration or letter to yourself as if you're putting on the crown again. What truth will you live by moving forward?

Reflection

_____

_____

_____

_____

_____

_____

_____

_____

Identity vs Reality

Closing Remarks

The crown is yours, and it's time to reclaim it. Walk in the fullness of your divine identity and purpose.

My prayer is that this is not just a reflection but treated as a **commission**, a bold **invitation to rise, walk in truth, and help others do the same.**

Rejection was never the end of your story—it was the soil where your roots grew deeper. You may have been mislabelled, misunderstood, or mishandled, but Heaven never lost sight of you.

God didn't just rescue you from rejection. He *reinstated* you. Not as a victim, but as royal; a priest, a carrier of His presence.

The crown isn't something you earn. It's what you were born with. You only forgot who you were but now you remember. And now that you know... it's time to walk in it.

So, what now?

1. **Wear your crown.** Everyday. Live like you are loved, chosen, and called. Speak what God says, even when your feelings say otherwise.
2. **Guard your identity.** Don't let life, people, or your past define you anymore. Return to the truth. Return to the Word.
3. **Help others reclaim their crown.** Share your story. Be a mirror that reflects God's love, truth, and grace. Become a restorer of broken crowns.

Your healing is not just for you; it's for everyone connected to your name.

The world doesn't need any more copycats. It needs **you:** fully free, boldly loved, and finally *aware of who you are.*

You are who God says you are.
You are crowned with purpose.
You are called and covered.
Welcome back to royalty!

Daily Identity Declaration

I am not rejected - I am royally chosen.

I am not broken - I am beautifully restored.

I am not who they said I was - I am who God says I am.

I carry glory, purpose, and power.

I wear my crown - and I walk like it.

In Jesus' name. Amen.

Identity Reset Affirmations

1.   I am chosen, not rejected.

"You are a chosen people, a royal priesthood, a holy nation, God's special possession..." **- 1 Peter 2:9**

1.   I am loved with an everlasting love.

"I have loved you with an everlasting love; I have drawn you with unfailing kindness." **- Jeremiah 31:3**

2.   God calls me by name. I am His.

"Fear not, for I have redeemed you; I have called you by name; you are mine." **- Isaiah 43:1**

4.   I am fearfully and wonderfully made.

"I praise you because I am fearfully and wonderfully made..." **- Psalm 139:14**

5.   I am accepted in the Beloved.

"To the praise of the glory of His grace, wherein He hath made us accepted in the beloved." - **Ephesians 1:6 (KJV)**

6. **I have been given authority and a royal inheritance.**

"The Spirit himself testifies... that we are God's children. Now if we are children, then we are heirs..." - **Romans 8:16–17**

7. **My past does not define me. I am a new creation.**

"Therefore, if anyone is in Christ, he is a new creation. The old has passed away..." - **2 Corinthians 5:17**

8. **I am not forgotten. I am engraved on His heart.**

"See, I have engraved you on the palms of my hands..." - **Isaiah 49:16**

9. **I am clothed in strength and dignity.**

"She is clothed with strength and dignity; she can laugh at the days to come." - **Proverbs**

31:25 (can apply to both men and women as spiritual royalty)

10. I was created for good works and divine purpose.

"For we are God's masterpiece... created in Christ Jesus to do good works..." **- Ephesians 2:10**

11. I have the mind of Christ.

"But we have the mind of Christ." **- 1 Corinthians 2:16**

12. I am no longer a slave to fear. I am a child of God.

"The Spirit you received does not make you slaves... but you received the Spirit of sonship." **- Romans 8:15**

13. God has crowned me with glory and honour.

"You made them a little lower than the angels and crowned them with glory and honour." **- Psalm 8:5**

14. I walk in freedom because I belong to Christ.

"So if the Son sets you free, you will be free indeed." - John 8:36

15. I am not forsaken. The Lord is with me.

"The Lord your God is with you, the Mighty Warrior who saves…" **- Zephaniah 3:17**

About the Author

Glacia Simpson is a Christian writer, speaker, host and creative visionary passionate about helping individuals embrace their God-given identity. She is the founder of Grace Creates, a faith-driven brand where creativity and purpose meet to inspire transformation. Glacia empowers women to heal from rejection, reclaim their worth, and walk boldly into purpose. Identity Vs Reality: Overcoming Rejection and Reclaiming Your Crown is her debut book, offering practical tools, journal prompts, and biblical wisdom to guide readers on a journey from brokenness to breakthrough.

Glacia lives in Jamaica, where she balances her work in media, production, ministry, and writing, always seeking to inspire others to discover the fullness of who God created them to be.

www.ingramcontent.com/pod-product-compliance
Lightning Source LLC
Chambersburg PA
CBHW071756090426
42737CB00012B/1839